# For God
# So Loved
# the World!

# Dedicated to
# Brooks Brigmon – God loves YOU!

For God So Loved the World, My John 3:16 Book

Copyright © Dandi Daley Mackall

Published by Thomas Nelson, Inc., P.O. Box 141000, Nashville, TN 37214.
www.thomasnelson.com

All rights reserved. No portion of this book may be reproduced, stored in a retrieval system, or transmitted in any form or by any means—electronic, mechanical, photocopy, recording, or any other—except for brief quotations in printed reviews, without the prior written permission of the publisher.

Unless otherwise noted, Scripture quotations are taken from The Holy Bible, New International Version® (NIV®).
Copyright © 1973, 1978, 1984 by International Bible Society. Used by permission of Zondervan. All rights reserved.

Library of Congress Cataloging-in-Publication Data [to come]
ISBN 13: 978-1-59145-524-0
ISBN 10: 1-59145-524-3

Printed in China

06 07 08 09 HH 9 8 7 6 5 4 3 2 1

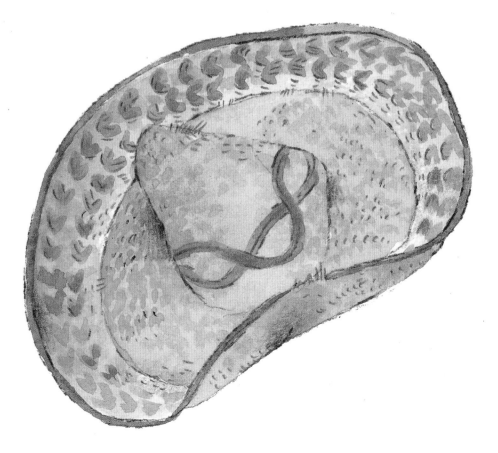

My John 3:16 Book

# For God
# So Loved
# the World!

By Dandi Daley Mackall

THOMAS NELSON PUBLISHERS
*Since 1798*

I can watch the clouds in a bright blue sky.

I can laugh at shapes that go floating by.

We have trees and flowers, and I'll tell you why . . .

For God so loved the world.

Para el Dios amó tan el mundo

(SPANISH)

9

We've got oceans filled with all kinds of fish.

On a moonlit night, hear them *swish, swish, swish.*

Then the stars come out like a giant wish,

For God so loved the world.

I aroha mai te Atua i to te ao

(TAHITIAN)

11

See the elephants and the giant cats?

Gorgeous, flying birds, scary, hanging bats.

From the big baboons to the tiny gnats—

For God so loved the world.

Olonim Feran Anaiye to fi omo bibi re da wa lolai

(NIGERIAN)

13

Ever wonder how God could make a dad,

Then create a mom from a rib? Not bad!

It was all a part of the plan God had,

For God so loved the world.

因為上帝如此愛世界
(CHINESE)

15

But the greatest gift that we got, by far,

Didn't come by plane, didn't come by car.

It was sent from heaven to where we are,

For God so loved the world.

Для богатак Полюбила Мир

(RUSSIAN)

17

For we all do things that we shouldn't do,

And we think bad thoughts without wanting to.

So God sent Jesus for me and you!

For God so loved the world.

そう世界愛される神のため

(JAPANESE)

19

Jesus lived on earth, but he came to die

'Cause he loved us so—that's the reason why.

Then he rose to heaven, though he's still nearby,

For God so loved the world.

Para o Deus amou assim o mundo

(PORTUGESE)

21

**W**hen you hear the truth, then you just believe.

And God's gift of Jesus, you just receive.

Then the love he gives you will never leave,

For God so loved the world.

For God so loved the world

(ENGLISH)

I am not alone. If I'm here or there,

I can talk to God anytime in prayer.

And I have a Friend who goes everywhere,

For God so loved the world.

Pour Dieu a ainsi aimé le monde

(FRENCH)

25

Para el Dios amó tan el mundo

(SPANISH)

I arona mai te Atua i to te ao

(TAHITIAN)

Olonim Feran Anaiye to fi omo bibi re da wa lolai

(NIGERIAN)

因為上帝如此愛世界

(CHINESE)

Для Бога Так Полюбил Мир

(RUSSIAN)

そう世界愛される神のため

(JAPANESE)

Para o Deus amou assim o mundo

(PORTUGESE)

Pour Dieu a ainsi aimé le monde

(FRENCH)

For God so loved the world

(ENGLISH)

All the world's a gift! Look around and see.

And the best Gift comes with a guarantee

That we'll be with God for eternity!

For God so loved the world.

# For God So Loved the World!

"For God so loved the world that he gave his
one and only Son, that whoever believes
in him shall not perish but have eternal life."

John 3:16, NIV